Oründ Awon Orisa

A Practitioner's Guide to Daily Devotion

Fayemi Abidemi Fakayode &
Obafemi Origunwa

DEDICATION

Iba Olódùmarè
Iba Ile a f'oko y'eri
Iba igba irunmole oju k'otun
Iba igba irunmola oju k'osi
Iba okanle ni erinwo irunmole
Iba Orunmila, eleri ipin
Iba Akoda
Iba Aseda
Iba Oluwo
Iba Ojugbona
Iba ori baba
Iba ori yeye
Iba ori inu
Iba adaiyeba.
Ase!

ACKNOWLEDGMENTS

We give sincere thanks to Olódùmarè for the blessing of Ifá, the intermediary of fate. It has been Òrunmìlà's wisdom that has guided us in this project from the very start. Our true intention is to provide a series of worship materials that will make the power and the wisdom of òrìsà lifestyle accessible and enjoyable to the world. Ase.

ABOUT THE AUTHORS

FAYEMI ABIDEMI FAKAYODE

BORN IN THE IFAJOYE/GBELEYI VILLAGE, IN
AKANRAN ONA ARA LOCAL GOVERNMENT,
NIGERIA, FAYEMI IS A DESCENDENT OF THE
LATE HIGH CHIEF PRIEST ABIDEMI ALABI

FAKAYODE. IN ACCORDANCE WITH PROTOCOL AND CUSTOM, HE WAS SENT TO LEARN IFA /ORISA IN THE COUMPOUND OF BABA OLATINWO OLOJAOKE. SINCE THEN, FAYEMI HAS BEEN INITIATED TO THE FOLLOWING SOCIETIES:

- IFA
- OGBONI
- ORISANLA
- EGUNGUN AND
- AWO ODE

FAYEMI BELIEVES THAT THE RELIGION OF ORISA IS THE ONLY ONE THAT CAN EXPLAIN TO YOU WHY YOU ARE HERE ON EARTH AND WHAT YOU CAME FOR, WHICH WILL DETERMINE WHAT WILL BE YOUR REPORT AFTER LIFE AND DEATH. UNLIKE COUNTERPART RELIGIONS, WHOSE PROPHETS WERE BORN THROUGH HUMAN BEINGS, ORISA ARE DIRECT PROPHETS THAT WERE NOT BORN THROUGH ORDINARY HUMANS.

FAYEMI DEDICATED HIMSELF TO THE ORIKI AWON ÒRÌSÀ PROJECT BECAUSE OF THE REALIZATION THAT MANY ORISA HAVE LONG VERSES OF ORIKI, BUT THE DEVOTEES DON'T

NECESSARILY KNOW THE MEANINGS OF THEM.
SO, KNOWING SHORT VERSES AND THEIR
MEANINGS IS PREFERABLE, ESPECIALLY FOR
OUR PEOPLE IN DIASPORA, WHO WILL BENEFIT
FROM KNOWING HOW TO PROPERLY RECITE
ORIKI. THIS ALONE WILL HELP THEM TO
RECEIVE GOODNESS AND BLESSING FROM
ÒRÌSÀ.

IF THERE IS ONLY OUTCOME OF THIS PROJECT,
IT WILL BE TO MAINTAIN THE HIGH QUALITY OF
ÒRÌSÀ WORSHIP, THROUGH PROPER
PRONOUNCIATION AND RECITATION OF ORIKI.

Obafemi Origunwa, MA
I have been a student of Orisa Lifestyle since
1992. In addition, I am a professionally-trained
counselor, with a Master of Arts in Education
with a concentration in Counseling from San
Diego State University. I am particularly
interested in Jungian psychology. And with a

Bachelor of Arts in Spanish Language & Literature from the University of California at Berkeley, I also enjoy total Spanish fluency. This particular combination of ancient wisdom and modern approach allows me to offer you a unique and refreshing blend of Western and Indigenous healing practices.

For over 15 years I have been working as a personal sustainability consultant. Through this experience I have learned strategies & techniques that generate extraordinary results for people from a broad range of backgrounds & philosophies. To date, I have helped over 50 thousand people develop personal rituals that energize their highest aspirations and inspire others to do the same. I invite you to contact me now to put my expertise to work for you.

For me, this project is one of the greatest investments into the spiritual and intellectual development of Òrìsà Lifestyle. I believe that millions of people will learn about and experience the wisdom of our tradition through the Oriki Awon Òrìsà series.

Contents

Yorùbá Ritual

Imagine a major intersection you know. Visualize the relentless flow of cars, buses, bikes and pedestrians, moving in all directions. Consider where all the travelers come from and where they go. The possibilities are endless. According to Yorùbá theology, the potential of the cross- roads is born out of èjiwàpò (twoness), hence the saying; "tako, tabo, èjiwàpò" (male, female, in together in two-ness). The crossroads produces exponential growth with infinite potential.

Each of the four cardinal points — North, South, East and West — embodies a transformative principle of ajo laiye (life's journey). These principles include birth, life, death and afterlife. Consequently, Yorùbá ritual drama continually reinforces the understanding that wherever these principles intersect, possibilities increase, awareness expands and we become conscious of Olódùmarè (God) at work. As devotees, our greatest imaginable challenge is to keep the mind and heart open to the full range of these possibilities, especially as we perform rituals and ceremonies. Otherwise, ritual without awareness is empty formality; lifeless and impotent.

In the beginning, when Obàtalà first traveled to the earth, he brought the principles of Existence from heaven contained in the Igbá Ìwà (Calabash of Existence) and placed them on the four cardinal points. In four phases, other òrìsàs joined him in the creation process. Each òrìsà was thereby made "owner" of one of the four days of Existence, and the "governor" of the transformative energy contained therein;

- Ojo Obàtalà/Osé: Obàtalà's day
- Ojo Awo/Ifá: Ifá's day

- Ojo Ogún: Ogún's day
- Ojo Sàngó/Jakuta: Sàngó's day

Generally speaking, a devotee refers to the holy day of her patron òrìsà as **ojo osé** (day of osé). It was Ifá that revealed to Obàtalà that there would be color associations, symbolic emblems, taboos, tutelary divinities and priestly rites particular to each of the four original days.

Òrìsà devotees gather to celebrate, share food, pray and consult the oracle every 4th day. This ritual is called "**Osé**". At dawn, the family begins cleaning the shrine and saluting the ancestors and the òrìsà, chanting **oríkì** and making offerings. Aesthetically, the shrine, chants and offerings are beautiful and inspirational to all who experience them, especially the divinities. Emotionally, chanting the oríkì evokes feelings of great pride, a sense of belonging and a heightened awareness of life's journey. Of equal importance, the oríkì also validate the devotees' faith by explicitly citing how each divinity is uniquely qualified – if not obliged – to guide and protect his or her "children" when we plead for assistance.

Osé is essential spiritual conditioning. In the same way that a musician's performance absolutely depends on practice, so must a devotee prepare herself to carry out her spiritual mission. Osé increases mental, emotional, and spiritual capacity. Osé builds stamina, develops discipline and reinforces the devotees' connection to the spirit world. The teachings shared during Osé sharpen the mind and soften the heart. In this way, Osé encourages the devotee to continually align herself with the will of Olódùmarè as it flows from heaven to earth and back.

In addition to its spiritual merits, however, it's important to recognize Osé as an ancient institution of great significance to the economic, political and social cohesion of the community. Accordingly, there are as many variations in the Osé ritual as there are Yoruba cultural regions. More specifically, the òrìsà tradition as we know it today, has evolved out of a synthesis between the Oduduwa dynasty and the various, local òrìsà practices. In practically every Yoruba kingdom, village and family lineage, this duality is conspicuously notable in the places of worship, in the local festivals and the king installation ceremonies. Everywhere, the iconography, oral traditions and ritual drama highlight the dual identity, which is locally based, yet linked to Ile Ife. In this way, it's important that we understand that what we now call Yoruba religion is actually a nomenclature given to a conglomeration of heterogeneous traditions. Collectively, these traditions espouse a plurality of beliefs and political histories, all of which are rooted in the innumerable deities, known as òrìsà, irunmole and ebora. Even so, everywhere the deities are known, the osé ritual is practiced and understood as an indispensible aspect Òrìsà Lifestyle.

In the pre-colonial eras, the òrìsà temples played an extremely important role in their respective communities. In many instances, the temple has historically been – and continues to be – a land owner, an organizer of rural and urban activities, a provider of educational, medical and cultural development and an equalizer of political power. More recently, the temple has become a viable symbol of Òrìsà Lifestyle around the world.

However, the temple, in and of itself, is not enough to symbolize Òrìsà Lifestyle. In actuality, it is the spiritual technologies and activities that take place inside the temple that make it a holy site, which functions as the hub of spirituality, sanctity and reverence. The sacred arts, in the form of song, dance, carvings, tapestries and murals all work together to enhance the act of worship and help to create a deep connection with one's internal spirit, the ancestors, the divinities and ultimately Olódùmarè.

Origin of the Osé Ritual

The sacred texts of Ifá teach us the importance of feeding the Òrìsà to obtain their favor and to achieve positive changes in our lives. A verse of the Holy Odù Irosun Osé clearly demonstrates how the practice was born. In this instance, Òrunmìlà was sent from heaven to earth to serve as a counselor, to interpret Ifá and to help humankind experience the Good Condition by avoiding life's dangers, pitfalls and perils. He was carrying out divination and sacrifice to redeem the lives of humanity. He also performed good works for men and their children. He cured to the sick, giving them hope, and bringing harmony to the areas of discord in their lives. All this he did without asking anything in exchange. Èsù noted that nobody thanked Òrunmìlà for his good deeds. Thus, he devised a plan with the Iyaami Osoronga - the powerful mothers.

During his own personal divination, Òrunmìlà learned about the pending arrival of some powerful people on earth. He consulted the oracle and determined that the Iyaami Osoronga would be sent to the world to wreak havoc in the lives of people who offered nothing in exchange for Òrunmìlà's work. This prompted Òrunmìlà to pay Olódùmarè a visit. En route, he met Iyaami Osoronga. Upon recognizing them, he asked the Iyaami about what he had seen in his divination. "Is it true that you are going to trouble the lives of humans?" When they confirmed, he ask them why. They replied "It is on account of the fact that you have refused to collect any payment for your services to the children of man. On account of this fact, the other divinities have been suffering hunger." Òrunmìlà recognized the gravity of the Iyaami Osoronga's words. He became perplexed because he did not want the sons of men to be punished. He did not want his work on earth and all his efforts to be destroyed. But at the same time, how could he allow the deities to go hungry? The powerful mothers notified Òrunmìlà that he should tell the inhabitants of earth that they should offer something to appease to the deities and to eliminate the hunger they had been suffering. They assured Òrunmìlà that if people complied with this they would be forgiven for their prior neglect.

Òrunmìlà returned home to consult Ifá and ask what could people offer to appease to the deities and to avoid losses. He was advised to offer obì – kola nut – which each person should place on the shrine of her respective deities to avoid calamities. Orúnmìlà began with his campaign, informing all of humanity to offer obì to ward off death, sickness, curses, losses and defeat. Thus it was that people began to offer obì to their deities and ancestors. This is a custom from ancient times that thrives into the present. Offering obì to the deities is a gesture to be forgiven for misdeeds, to pacify the deities and to avert attacks from the Iyaami Osoronga.

The Power of Worship

If you only have one Òrìsà Lifestyle Agreement in your entire life, let it be worship. Worship is the most essential element of spiritual development and personal greatness. Stated differently, when you worship, you are actually conditioning many of the activities associated with a highly cultivated intuition, as well as a clearly defined sense of purpose. More specifically, the act of worship sets the stage for you to pray, meditate, chant, sing, play music, dance, divine, perform sacrifice, participate in ceremonies, festivals and so on.

Each one of these practices is essential to your spiritual development because they activate the body, heart, mind and soul. For example, something as simple as prayer becomes very powerful over time. The intensity of your prayer in an emergency is likely to be much greater than when everything is flowing nicely. Several years ago, when I was just starting to see clients, I went outside my house to see that my car had been stolen. Immediately, I started to think of all the important things I could not do without my car. But as my anxiety grew, something interesting happened: I went straight to the shrine to ask Ifá. The Odù directed me to appease my mother's spirit. The offering was relatively small, consisting of foodstuffs from my own kitchen. I did as instructed, then called the police to file a report. Within 4 hours my car was returned. After the fact, I reflected upon the intensity and focus of my prayers that day. Before then, I had been performing my rituals with sincerity, but I lacked a real sense of urgency. However, after that experience, I learned to make every prayer as if someone's life depended upon it.

So, the more you pray – under varying circumstances and conditions – the more reverent and humble you become towards the power that sustains the universe, Olódùmarè. Intellectually, prayer also sets the stage for meditation. It has been said that prayer is invoking the spirit and meditation is listening to the spirit.

Similarly, anyone who can sing, dance and clap at the same time, will tell you that it requires some concentration and focus. Osé rituals are almost always defined by the combination of prayer, song, clapping and motion. More importantly, when people engage in this particular combination of activities, they often reach an ecstatic state of consciousness or even full possession, both of which are ways to make direct connections with the divine.

Framework: Yoruba Calendar

The Yoruba week has four days:

- Ojo kinni osé - First Day: Obàtalà, Yemoo, Ori, Èsù, +
- Ojo Keji - Second Day: Òrunmìlà, Osun, Ori, Èsù, +

- Ojo Keta - Third Day: Ogún, Osoosi, Ori, Èsù, +
- Ojo Kerin - Fourth Day: Sango, Oya, Ori, Èsù, +

It is on these worship days that people collectively and individually focus upon the source of life itself. At the same time, the worship days are the time for you, as a devotee, to actively seek out your personal core and learn from the inside out: During worship, you ask the deep questions about who you are, where you're from and what you're destined to do. And the best part is that, if you pay attention, you will also get deep answers during worship.

On a larger scale, each òrìsà has its own annual festival, even Ori – one's personal destiny. The Ori kadun festival has a lot in common with the Western concept of a birthday celebration. In Yoruba, Ori kadun literally means "my head, or being has revolved round the year." This is a festival that celebrates your personal providence, ori. So, Ori Kadun is all about counting your blessings in a ritual manner. It is by virtue of the rites involved in performing the Ori Kadun festival that you increase your awareness of your own sacred authority.

Before you recite your personal Odù, or any Odù, for that matter, you must learn to commune with your own internal spirit. Long before you become an initiate of an òrìsà society, you must know how to venerate your ancestors properly. Anything else is putting the proverbial cart before the horse. Ifá tells us in the Holy Odù Ogunderin, that:

One's mother is one's divinity,
One's father is one's divinity,
One's internal spirit is one's divinity,
One's sacred text is one's divinity...
We venerate the ancestors before the òrìsà.

So part of the reason why worship is such a high impact Òrìsà Lifestyle Agreement is because it actively aligns you with those spiritual and personal forces that are closest and most familiar to you. This is where the deep, emotional connection is strongest. This is where the learning is most personal, most meaningful. For this reason, the home is considered the original temple and worship is its foundation.

Daily Devotion & Patterns of Spiritual Maturity

Let us not engage the world hurriedly
Let us not grasp the rope of wealth impatiently
That which should be treated with mature
judgment
Let us not deal with in a state of anger
When we arrive at a cool place
Let us rest fully
Let us give continuous attention to the future
And let us give deep consideration
to the consequences of things
And this is because of our eventual passing
- Holy Odu EjiOgbe

Knowledge feeds the ego and thus promotes arrogance and delusions of grandeur. Furthermore, the more knowledge the ego seeks, the more frustrated it becomes. Or, in the words of Edo Babláwo, Eziza Ogiemwanye, "even if you sweep all day long, you will not have enough to fill the well." Similarly, the ego can never be fulfilled, especially not by the consumption of knowledge. More precisely, knowledge is perilous to spiritual development for two reasons:

1. Knowledge causes you to draw conclusions: This is contrary to spirit because reality is constantly changing. As a result, the knowledge brokers are constantly scrambling impatiently to keep up with the "latest, freshest, newest" information. But alas, their efforts are all in vain. Invariably, today's knowledge will become tomorrow's folly, as obsolete as last year's cell phone technology.

2. Knowledge promotes detail complexity: This is an effective way to dissect and identify many variables. One terrible side effect of detail complexity, however, is that, the more adept you become at it, the more you lose sight of the forest for the trees. Consequently, the knowledge brokers and consumers tend to

know everything except for the real purpose and reason for having such information.

In this way, those who are driven by the quest for knowledge eventually get lost in a world of empty materialism and gross misunderstanding of divine purpose.

In the verse above, Ifá teaches us to see the world from the perspective of truth, which is eternal and unchanged from one millennia to the next. The sacred texts – which reflect keen observation of the cosmos, the ecology and the human spirit – have remained unchanged for tens of thousands of years. Consequently, everyday, science gets closer and closer to the original observations and discoveries made by ancient man.

Daily devotion destroys the falsehood of temporal knowledge by training the devotee to be reborn in the truth of eternal life. When we read "Let us give continuous attention to the future. And let us give deep consideration to the consequences of things. And this is because of our eventual passing," this is a call to worship. It implies that those who live by knowledge alone will die when their knowledge dies. But those who live by the principles of creation will realize the Good Condition and enjoy everlasting life with Olódùmarè (Holy Odu IrosunIwori).

Daily devotion is a simple, 7-step method of prayer and meditation that destroys the false premises of temporal knowledge by leading you deeper into the pattern through which your personal destiny unfolds. Whereas knowledge promotes attention to detail complexity, devotion aligns your body, heart, mind and spirit with pattern complexity. Pattern complexity is concerned with the dynamic interplay between subtle influences that produce slow, long term effects. Stated differently, attention to pattern complexity conditions you to become increasingly aware of "things that like to occur together" as opposed to "things that cause other things to occur". For example, age does not cause puberty to happen. Likewise, puberty does not cause one to age. In reality, they coincide with one another, according to a pattern of dynamic complexity that is unique to each individual.

Life unfolds in overlapping spheres. But the logic of language only allows us to explain life in linear, sequential terms. Daily devotion promotes systems awareness that broadens your sensitivity to the reciprocal flow of influence between physical and metaphysical realities. Nothing is ever influenced in a single direction: heaven touches earth and earth touches heaven as well. Ifá says:

There is no pregnant woman
who cannot give birth to a babalawo
There is no woman who cannot give birth to
Òrunmìlà himself
If a father begets a child,
however long it might take,
the child can also give birth to the father.
If a mother gives birth to a child,
she can still be reborn by that same child
This was Ifá's teaching to Òrunmìlà who said,
I shall bring heaven to earth
and earth to heaven
- Holy Odù IworiWodi

It is precisely this interplay of reciprocal influence that you will come to understand through regularly practicing daily devotion, which we call the Osé Ritual. For these reasons and more, true adepts consider the Osé Ritual the bedrock of Òrìsà Lifestyle.

The Healing Power of Devotion

Devotion implies prolonged focus and concentrated effort. Unlike love, which is purely emotional and highly subjective, devotion explicitly requires direct action. I know a woman, for example, who loves her husband with all of her heart. Still, in spite of that truth, she will never devote her life to "the cause" of loving him. Why? Because she is devoted to herself, her dreams and her freedom. As the saying goes, you cannot serve two causes at once without compromising both, as well as your own personal integrity.

Before you can be truly devoted, you have to know, beyond the shadow of a doubt, the answer to this simple question; "Who do you serve?" Carl Jung tells us that people are born to serve the Divine; that each of us is born with an irresistible need to serve God. More importantly, even in the absence of a well-defined image of God, the individual psyche will borrow images and motifs from the Ancestral Memory and create a god-like figure. Through dream analysis, Jung detailed some notable tendencies that defied the logic of the rational mind.

"Out of the purely personal form of the dreams, develop an archaic god-image that is infinitely far from the conscious idea of God… We are dealing with a genuine and thoroughly primitive god-image that grew up in the unconscious of a civilized person and produced a living effect – an effect which might well give the psychologist of religion food for reflection. There is nothing about this image that could be called personal: it is a wholly collective image, the ethnic origin of which has long been known to us… We are dealing with a reactivated archetype… It is not a question of inherited ideas, but of inherited thought -patterns."

These thought patterns, or archetypes, are expressed as the òrìsà. More precisely, it is through the òrìsà lifestyle that we see the highest culmination of archetypal ideals. For devotees, archetypes have become more than idealizations of of human nature. It is a religion, which facilitates the art of life. Without an ounce of dogma, the òrìsà lifestyle promotes devotion to purity and refinement. As is consistent with the mandates of my own destiny, as dictated by the Holy Odù IrosunOse, the virtues and mysteries of òrìsà lifestyle are revealed through performance of the Osé ritual.

To be certain, Osé is a sacred rite, through which the priest and the worshippers join together to recreate the conditions in which òrìsà devotion was first revealed by the deities themselves. The shrine serves as an urban oasis, where weary travelers meet and eat from the communal pot of spiritual nourishment. And while much of this nourishment consists of actual foodstuffs, like yams, palm oil, gin, kola nuts and so on, there is a considerable amount of visual feasting as well. The Òrìsà shrine is typically a repository of Yoruba sculpture. Each divinity is represented in elaborately carved wooden statues, as well as bronze moulds and iron works. These images, called iworan, are placed near the shrine of the òrìsà in question. Consequently, at the doorway, it is typical to see an image of Èsù, the heavenly gatekeeper and arbiter of ritual energy. Thus, from the time one enters into the shrine, the ceremony has begun and Osé rituals unfold as an improvised drama whose plot is woven out of the divination, the mythological stories and personal testimonials. That is, the combination of colors and tastes, juxtaposed against the syncopated sounds of handclaps, chants and sacred rattles creates an undisturbed harmony between the participants and the divine forces. Thus, the stage is set for devotion.

Spiritual Journey:

Building Community through Ritual & Ceremony

From saying prayers before dinner, to telling bedtime stories, to blowing out birthday candles, rituals create and reinforce memories. At its core, memory is the recollection of our divine origins[1]. That is, when a child is conceived, there is a rhythmic force that causes his physical body to "member" itself, one organ at a time. Then, once the child is born, the same force that caused him to "member" himself in embryo causes him to consciously and deliberately "re-member" the heavenly source

---

[1] It should come as no surprise, then that the term religion is rooted in the latin word, *religare* to restrain, tie back, which connotes the process of tying people back to the heavenly origins of humanity.

of his earthly mission. Hence, the babaláwo prays, *èmi kò gbódò sùn píyè*, "I must not lose the power to remember." Rituals like naming, rites of passage, marriage and burial punctuate the cycle of life by creating and reinforcing memories. Like good music, good food, and great stories, rituals conjure intense personal feelings and consolidate collective consciousness at the same time. Stated simply, rituals build community. In the pages that follow, we shall explore Yorùbá ritual as a means for building community:

Iba igba irunmole ijokotun
pay homage to the 200 divinities seated to the right
Iba igba irunmole ijokosi
pay homage to the 200 divinities seated to the left
Iba okanlenireinwo irunmole
pay homage to the 401 divinities

      The invocation above does not reflect defective mathematics. To the contrary, it is essential to understanding the ability of Yorùbá people to integrate new ideas and yet remain consistent with their cultural heritage at the same time. Traditional Yorùbá thought can be characterized as a "Plus 1 Philosophy", which fundamentally reminds us that, while there are certainly two sides to every story, there is also a third possibility, a new paradigm that redefines everything that existed prior. So, the two hundred divinities to the right, and the two hundred divinities to left represent known forces. Together, however, they become four hundred divinities, plus one. According to proverbial wisdom, *"Àgbààgbà méjì ló mo ídì éta,* two elders know the meaning of three. Here, the implication is that 'Two implies three,' or 'In two is contained the third.' The third factor here stands not merely for the number three, but for an unknown factor, an entity beyond our measure, the fact of fate, the unpredictable 'X.'"[2] This third factor can be called the law of continuity. It is the intangible link between objects, space and time. Consider, for example, that each of us has an outer experience – what we see, hear and feel. This outer experience is shared by all who are exposed to it. At the same time, however, we also have an inner experience – what we think, sense and intuit. This inner experience is completely unseen by others. More

---

[2] Okediji, The Shattered Gourd. Page 7

importantly, even though the inner and outer experiences are distinct, separate and sometimes contradict one another, the existence of one neither precludes, nor invalidates the existence of the other. Instead, they coexist simultaneously within a single individual. In this way, the inner self is inextricably linked to the outer self. Through the interplay between inner and outer experience the web of human consciousness is woven. So, whereas dualistic thinking emphasizes "either-or", Yorùbá traditional thought emphasizes "both and". It is wonderfully exemplified by the Holy Odù Iwori-Ofun which tells the story of two best friends who visited a Babaláwo for consultation. The friends were advised to make a sacrifice in order to preserve their friendship. They had more faith in the strength of their relationship than the predictions of Ifá. They refused to perform the sacrifice. Esu, who is the messenger of the gods and the carrier of sacrifices, heard of this. Naturally, he decided to test their theory. One day, as the two unsuspecting friends were walking side by side, enjoying one another's conversation and good company, Esu walked in between them, wearing a hat that was white on one side and black on the other. They both commented on the odd fellow they had just seen, but disagreed on the color of his hat. One swore the hat was white. The other was certain that it was black. Because both were absolutely sure of what they had seen, and because each described something so completely opposite what the other had seen, each friend felt justified in insisting that the other was mistaken. Back and forth they argued, each volley intensifying their respective convictions. The disagreement escalated into a scuffle, which ended their friendship on the spot.[3] The reality is, of course, that the hat was both white and black. The ability to see both extremes, as well as the golden thread that links them is the law of continuity.

The discovery of continuity, or the union of all things, is the objective of Yorùbá ritual. That is, we use ritual to eliminate our sense of separateness. The elimination of separateness does not, however, imply a loss of

---

3

http://www.awostudycenter.com/Articles/art_what_is_esu.htm

identity. To the contrary, it means complete realization of one's eternal identity. Ifá divination and sacrifice, for example, is only concerned with helping a person to harmonize his or her *orí odé* (outer physical experience) with his or her *orí inú* (destiny). Again, this reflects the understanding that the physical experience is a reflection of what is happening on the metaphysical plane, expressed as *inú*.

In terms of structure and format, Yorùbá ritual can be thought of as the dramatization of cosmic riddles. When the universe poses these riddles, they manifest on the earthly plane as changes that create crises and problems, as well as opportunities and abundance. When it is most effective, ritual allows a person to actually enter into the riddles and relive the solutions that were discovered by the ancient sages so many hundreds of generations ago. Ritual drama then, is a return to the conditions of original discovery. With the cosmic stage set, rituals allow worshippers to directly experience the riddle and its solution, according to the example that was set in ancient times. Hence, the proverb that reminds us; *e jé ká seé bí wón ti nseé, k'ó le rí b'ó ti nrí*, 'let's do it as they do it [as it ought to be done] so that it turns out as it is ought to'. Here, a distinction must be made between Yorùbá ritual tradition and the spiritual power it intends to harness. Whereas the tradition is perpetuated through conservatism (i.e., the minimization of change), spiritual power is perpetuated though dynamism (i.e., the maximization of change). Conceptually, the relation between tradition and spirit can be likened to the relationship between a glass and the water it contains. The glass – like tradition- is most effective when it remains unbroken. The water – like spirit – contained in the glass however, is meant to flow. All the same, "the Yorùbás are not ruled by timeless traditions – but, like any people – have, make and write their own history in different idioms and registers and from multiple perspectives."[4]

Consequently, Yorùbá ritual drama unfolds spontaneously, in direct relation to the imperatives of physical, political, economic and historical realities. So, even though the Yorùbá descendents of Cuba, Brazil, Haiti and the United States share a common point of reference, their rituals manifest and become real as the practitioners actually experience

---

[4] Apter, Andrew. Black Critics and Kings. Page 1

them in different places and times. "The notion is that patterns from the past, when restored through performance, establish the terms on which the desired consequences can be negotiated... These formulas then become models for present practice that permit a wide range for interpretation and representation."[5] Ultimately, as we are able to accept the deeper truths of the òrìsà teachings, we come to understand that all forms of separation are contrary to God-consciousness. This is the significance of the proverb that says "No matter how far a river flows, it cannot forget its source."

---

[5] Thompson Drewal, Margaret. Yoruba Ritual. Page 91

Ritual: Sacrifice

Yorùbá ritual is firmly rooted in and contextualized by the coded language of mythology. More concretely, the principles of creation are codified into formulas, expressed as axioms, proverbs, incantations, poetry and myths. This coded language and the principles it expresses come to life through the performance of rituals, ceremonies and festivals. The encyclopedia for all such knowledge and performance is contained in the Odù Ifá. As such, within the sacred verses of Ifá, we find the archetypal[6] stories that give meaning to

---

[6] All human beings share a collective unconscious. Inside all human beings there are certain patterns of behavior. These patterns are elements in the personality which are

practically every Yorùbá ritual, from courtship to burial. Most significantly, however, the principles exist as pure potential, incapable of becoming manifest until they are activated and brought to life through ritual. Of all Yorùbá rituals, sacrifice is considered the most effective. So, whereas Ifá is the word of creation, sacrifice ritually empowers the word, activating it and reactivating it in different places and times.

Many verses of Ifá emphasize the Yorùbás' faith in the healing power of sacrifice. Hence, proverbial wisdom advises us, *riru ebo ni gbe ni, airu ebo ni ki gbeniyan,* making of sacrifice favors one; refusal to sacrifice benefits no one. Once again, we turn to the Fon of Dahomey for a deeper understanding of why sacrifice is so effective: "The blood contains *ye* [and for this reason] the life force of one entity is transferable to another, either through ritual or blood line... The *ye* as a source of transferential and transformative power shares,

---

innate and universal. Universal archetypes are the symbols that every child has the potential to create, regardless of race, creed or culture. Archetypes are aspects of the human personality and are frequently found in literature and myth.

in this way, qualities of a mask through which the identity of one is enveloped in that of another." [7] When we perform sacrificial rites, therefore, the goal is to deliberately draw metaphysical energy into the physical realm, using it to empower and sanctify otherwise crude, physical objects. These objects, in turn, function as portals of communication between worlds. "Ritual specialists bring that which is normally inaccessible, unseen, or imagined, into the phenomenal world, where it can be observed and contemplated."[8] In this way, ritual seeks to restore balance and harmony between the physical and metaphysical realms.

Many times, sacrificial rituals culminate by depositing the offering at the *orita*, commonly referred to as the crossroads. Orita, however, also denotes "confluence" or "junction." It is a point where things meet, coincide, collide and conclude. It is the place where the teachings conjoin with the realities of everyday life. Still, in spite of its importance as the portal for spiritual contact, the orita is only the catalyst for an even deeper insight, a flash

---

7 Blier, Suzanne Preston. African Vodun Page 194

[8] Thompson Drewal, Margaret. Yoruba Ritual. Page 90

of the spirit that illuminates the spark of creative genius that Olódùmarè breathed into each and every individual at the moment of inception. As such, the orita facilitates a sudden glimpse of something that comes together because two or more aspects of all experience are suddenly and surprisingly unified in space in time. At that moment, there is an explosion of awareness, as otherwise mundane facts coalesce into a single truth, revealing the unity of all things.

Ritual: Making Ose

Because sacrifices are made complete when offerings are deposited at the crossroads, Yorùbá ritual protocol continually reinforces the understanding that wherever paths intersect possibilities increase and awareness expands. This is only possible, however, because each of the four directions – North, South, East and West – embodies a distinct principle of the creation cycle. These principles include birth, lifespan, death and rebirth. Similarly, these same principles can be expressed as light, physics, darkness and metaphysics. In either case, together, they represent phases of transformation and ascent. More significantly, when Yorùbá devotees allow this understanding of transformation and purification to inform the way we perform rituals and ceremonies, we gain access to the deeper truths of worship. Furthermore, the transformative power of this four part ritual cycle is captured and indexed by the traditional Yorùbá worship week, which consists of four days. Each day is dedicated to the veneration of a particular cluster of òrìsàs.

In the beginning, when *Obàtalà* first traveled to the earth, he brought the four principles of creation from heaven contained in the *Igba Iwa* (Calabash of Existence) and placed them on the four cardinal points. In turn, other òrìsàs joined Obàtalà in the creation process. As a result, each òrìsà was made "owner" of one of the four days of the original Yorùbá week, which is as follows;

- Ojo Ogún (Ogún's day)
- Ojo Sàngó/Jakuta (Sàngó's day)
- Ojo Obatala/Osé (Obatala's day)
- Ojo Awo/Ifá (Ifá's day)

Generally speaking, a worshipper refers to the holy day of his or her patron òrìsà as *ojo ose* (e.g., osé Ifá). It was Ifá who revealed to Obàtalà that there would be color associations, symbolic emblems, taboos, tutelary divinities and priestly rites particular to each of the four original days. This revelation served as the framework for the Yorùbá worship week, which we have observed since antiquity. For this reason, Orúnmìlà became known as the "owner of all four days created by *Obàtalà*":

Ifá ló lòní

Ifá ló lòla

Ifá ló lòtunla pèlú è

Orúnmìlà lò nijó mérèèrin Òòsá dá'áyé...[9]

So, in the case of Ifá priests and devotes, worshippers gather to celebrate, share food, pray and consult the oracle every fourth day.[10]

---

[9] Ogunda Meji: See Abimbola, Wande. An Exposition of Ifá. Page 170.

[10] This is commonly referred to as every five days, according to the Nigerian counting system. But

This ritual is called "making *osé*." At dawn, everyone is expected to begin cleaning the shrine and saluting the òrìsà with chants and ritual offerings. Aesthetically, the shrine, chants and offerings are meant to be a thing of beauty and joy to all who experience them, especially the òrìsà. Emotionally, chanting the oríkì in honor of the òrìsà and the ancestors invokes feelings of great pride, a sense of belonging and a connection to a power greater than oneself. Of equal importance, the chants also validate the devotees' faith in the òrìsà by explicitly citing how the divinity is uniquely qualified – if not obliged – to guide and protect his or her "children" when we plead for their assistance.

"The practical logic of òrìsà worship rests on a straightforward principle of reciprocal exchange. Propitiation of the deities – by individuals or communities – is strategic action to attain specific ends."[11] According to tradition, "to whom much is given, much is expected." So, in the case of making osé, the divinities, who

---

numerically, if the ose day falls on the 4th, the next ose will be on the 8th, the 12th, the 16th and do on.

[11] Apter, Andrew. Black Critics and Kings. Page 98

receive the devotees' offerings, prayers and praise, are also expected to lend tremendous support to individual endeavors. Here, the importance of self interest cannot be overstated. Making ose emphasizes personal growth, authentic happiness, and general well-being. Making ose invites the devotee to ritually recall his or her core values and to proactively create positive change in his or her life. A basic understanding of making ose is that as a person takes care of himself, he will be in a much better position to take care of the environment, the community, and the members of his family. With such a sound spiritual foundation, the devotee will certainly be in a much better position for the *òrìsà* to support him in the process of realizing his spiritual identity. Making osé is, therefore, personal worship. When making osé, the devotee is making explicit efforts to improve life for himself, his family and his loved ones. He is motivated primarily by the quest for those resources that will allow him to feel good and satisfy his immediate needs. In turn, the devotee, who has received great support from the divinities, is likewise expected to continue to give offerings, prayers and praise to the unseen forces that facilitate individual success.

Public Ceremony &
Social Change: Odun

Observance of the four day worship calendar allows the individual devotee to create a virtual crossroads of protective spiritual energy. By "visiting" this intersection every four days, the devotee cultivates a strong rapport with the òrìsà. Through this rapport, he gradually and eventually aligns himself with the very principles of creation. In this way, the devotee is proactive about his own spiritual conditioning. Making osé is, in this sense, an important spiritual exercise because it increases the individual's capacity for self mastery.[12] At the same time, however, there always exists a danger that, as the individual's spiritual power increases, his overall social capacity will actually decrease. "In making him more self-reliant, it may make him more self-sufficient; it may lead to aloofness and indifference. It often makes an individual so insensitive in his relations to others as to develop an illusion of being really able to stand and act alone - an unnamed form of insanity which is responsible for a large part of the remedial suffering in the world."[13] So, whereas osé represents the individual pursuit of spiritual well being, there is also a form of collective worship that works directly for the common good. This collective worship is called *odún* (annual festival). Odún brings together all the members of the community to perform public ceremonies. There are odún for everything, from the municipal òrìsà to the spirits of deceased warriors, to the onset of the

---

[12] Holy Odù Ogbe Atè says, in part: Now, after I had been initiated I will complement it with self initiation. All those things that are my taboos, I will surely avoid them. I have been initiated. I will now reinitiate myself. See Falade, Fasina. Ifá, The Key to its Understanding. Page 43

[13] Dewey, John. Democracy of Education. Page 44

harvest season. And while these ceremonies certainly do empower individuals (such as kings, chiefs and devotees) they do so with the specific intent to address collective needs. "Annual òrìsà festivals propitiate town deities for the public good. In the past, town deities were invoked for protection against slave raids and attacks by neighbors. Today the outside menace may be the federal government... The principal task of public ritual is to harness the power which rages in the outside world by transporting it from the surrounding bush into the center of town, where it can purify the community."[14]

One of the most significant, historical examples of the purifying effects of public ceremony is recalled every August in Haiti, commemorating the *Bois Caiman* ceremony. Bois Caiman (pronounced *BWAH*-ky-mahn) is the site of the public ritual presided over by *Boukman Dutty* and *Cecile Fatiman* on August 14, 1791. During the ceremony, a priestess of Ogún was possessed by the spirit of justice, and confirmed *Boukman* and others as leaders of what would become known as the **Haitian**

---

[14] Apter, Andrew. Black Critics and Kings. Page 98

Revolution. To be certain, the Haitian Revolution was and still is the most successful war waged by Africans on either side of the Atlantic.[15] More than 150 years before any African nation achieved independence from the European colonizers, the Revolution established Haiti as a free black republic, the first of its kind. In fact, the Haitian Revolution was the single greatest inspiration for the Latin American Wars of Independence. The following prayer, attributed to *Boukman,* was recited at the Bois Caiman ceremony:

Bon Dje ki fè la tè. Ki fè soley ki klere nou enro.

"The God who created the earth; who created the sun that gives us light.

Bon Dje ki soulve lanmè. Ki fè gronde loray.

The God who holds up the ocean; who makes the thunder roar.

Bon Dje nou ki gen zorey pou tande.

Our God who has ears to hear.

Ou ki kache nan niaj. Kap gade nou kote ou ye la.

---

[15] Only the Aduwa War of Ethiopia remotely compares but still does not quite measure up to the significance of the Haitian Revolution.

You who are hidden in the clouds; who watches us from where you are.

Ou we tout sa blan fè nou sibi.

You see all that the white man has made us suffer.

Dje blan yo mande krim.

The white man's god asks him to commit crimes.

Bon Dje ki nan nou an vle byen fè.

But the God within us wants to do good.

Bon Dje nou an ki si bon, ki si jis, li ordone vanjans.

Our God, who is so good, so just, He orders us to revenge our wrongs.

Se li kap kondui branou pou nou ranpote la viktwa.

It's He who will direct our arms and bring us the victory.

Se li kap ba nou asistans.

It's He who will assist us.

Nou tout fet pou nou jete potre dje Blan yo ki swaf dlo lan zye.

We all should throw away the image of the white man's god who is so pitiless.

Koute vwa la libète kap chante lan kè nou.

Listen to the voice for liberty that speaks in all our hearts.[16]

Here, we see how the Haitians have quite masterfully organized public ceremony for sweeping social change. In keeping with Yorùbá public ceremonies in West Africa, the sacred background of Bois Caiman functions more as a catalyst than a dominating feature. The religious and spiritual dimensions of the ceremony activate and validate mythic concepts – primarily having to do with òrìsà Ogún, better known in Haiti as *Ogou*. "The Ogou operate in extreme social situations – in difficult, trying, perilous times – and so the strength they exhibit in themselves and call forth in their devotees is the strength of someone pushed to the limit... Ogou is a protective weapon for those who serve him... because Ogou taps the deepest source of human energy: anger, the final defiant refusal to admit defeat... In situations of oppression then, to touch one's anger is to reclaim one's power, position, and

---

[16] www.wikipedia.com

dignity in the world."[17] So, in the case of the Bois Caiman ceremony, Ogún's mythological force gives a deeper spiritual meaning to the conflict, the conquest, and the conciliation of the African collective over the French colonizers. Still, what is most important to understand is that the mythological story makes the ceremony meaningful precisely because of the socio-political changes it created. For this reason, one characteristic that distinguishes public ceremony from private ritual is that the element of social change is more fully pronounced.[18]

Similarly, as anyone who has attended the Òsún Festival in Òsogbo can attest, the festival is a clear demonstration of the òrìsà's power to mobilize the masses. As it is in Haiti, Brazil and elsewhere in the Yorùbá world, said ability is premised almost entirely on the divinities' proven ability to facilitate real improvement in the community at large. In Òsogbo, for example, the entire Òsún grove would have been completely razed by loggers,

[17] Barnes, Sandra. Africa's Ogun. Page 73

[18] Ajayi, Omofolabo. Seimiotics of Yoruba Dance. Page 58-59

developers and realtors – as has already happened to virtually all other sacred groves of Yorùbá land – if not for Òsún's enduring powers.[19] Not only is there still a grove, but it is lovely, befitting Òsún - matron of the arts and curator of all things beautiful. It is an expansive complex of artistically decorated garden shrines, nestled quietly into the forest, along the banks of the profoundly tranquil Òsún river. Thus, those who enter – regardless of their ethnic, national or religious backgrounds – feel a direct sense of connection to the òrìsà. People who bathe in Òsún's waters or allow themselves to be swept up in the river of spontaneous dance that flows throughout the grove leave the festival with direct experiences of having communed with the divinity herself. In this way, the odún provides a breadth of spiritual empowerment that no single individual is capable of giving to the masses of people. Instead, the power that lives in the sacred grove, and manifests itself during the public ceremony can only be channeled through the community's shared consciousness.

---

[19] Abodunrin, Femi. Character is Beauty. Page 27

Oriki Awon Òrìsà

Elédùmarè

Kiki	*Kabiesi eledumare*
	Your highness, Elédùmarè
Orin	*Kabiesi ooooooo*
	Your highness
	Edùmarè eeeee, Olorun ajuba re ooo x2
	Edùmarè I pay you homage x2
	Oba ti ko lorogun o
	The king who has no rival
	Oba ti ko loba kan o
	The king without competitors
	Edumare lorun ajuba re
	Edùmarè is the king we to whom we pay homage
Oríkí	*Olodumare oba agbanla aye*
	King of the world
	Olodumare oba alafunfun gbo ooo

King of purity

Pani pani ti jinni

One who kills and awakens

Oba ibere oba opin

King of the beginning and the end

Oba iwaju oba eyin

King of what is before and behind

Oba oni Oba ola oba titi lailai

King of today, tomorrow and forever
Oba ti oda imole bora bi aso

King wrapped with light like cloth
Monimoni ko to dani

He who knows one before creation

Oba ogbagba ti gba alaini ara

King who helps and favors the lonely
Olo kiki isenbaye

The famous one of antiquity

Èsù

Kiki   *Akinboru*

One we invoke when making sacrifice
Akinboye

One we invoke when sacrifice is being accepted

Akin ibosise

One we invoke when sacrifice is manifesting

Orin   *Abisoso Abe X2*

Unless the razor blade sharpens

Bakere o lorunkun ejo

Baakere never kneels for crime

Abisoso abe

Unless razor blade sharpens

Esu odara o lori a gbe Erule ooo

Esu Odara has no head for carrying loads

Abisoso abe

Unless razor blade sharpens

Baake Baba moje n rejo laalu

Baake please don't let me have any court case

Bara moje n rejo

please don't let me have any court case

Pakuta mewa

One who eats beans together with sand
Bara moje n rejo

please don't let me have any court case

Oríkí   *Esu laalu*

Èsù Laalu

Ogiri oko

Wall of stones

Oni panti oko

One who has dusty stones

Agbenu ile so ogo sode

He who stays inside and throws the back of his head outside

Agbode sogo si ile

He who stay outside and throws the back of his head inside

Esu odara tanni komo pe iwo loni panti oko

Esu odara who doesn't know that it is you who has dusty stones

Agbenu ile soko soja

One at home who throws stones into the market

Agboja soko sinu ile

One at market who throws stones to the house

O ba elekunsunkun keru o ba elekun

He helps somebody who is crying

to cry until the crier is afraid

Elekun n sunkun laroye sun eje

While somebody is crying, Laroye is weeping blood

Oba onimi su mi keru o ba onimi

He helps one defecating to defecate

Oni mi nsu mi laroye sun ifun

while someone defecates Laroye is vomiting his intestines

Egungun

Kiki   *Ele: gbogbo moriwo tuwole wooo*

Call: All deveotees of egungun respond iwooooo!

Egbe: iwo oooo!

Response: iwo ooooo!

Ele: gbingbin

Call: Panting

Egbe: kin

Response: Kin! (sound of affirmation)

Ele: eru

Call: Baggage (load, responsibility, burden, etc)

Egbe: òwò

Response: Money!

Orin   *Egungun olowo legungun wa*

Our egungun is one of the richest

ororisa olomo lawa n tele

We follow our begotten orisa

E telewa kalo kale romo gbejo

Follow us and get your own children to dance with us

Modaso fegun moda ibora si x2

I make a cloth for egungun with fabric x2

Omo elegun ki jaje tan

A child of egungun always saves money

Modaso fegun moda ibora si

I make a cloth for egungun with its wrapping fabric

Oriki   *Egungun abala*

Egungun, the commanding one with trailing cloth

Arago gbale

Heavenly being

Ara orun kin in kin

Being from the barrel

Ara idi agba

Being from the hole

Egungun ara abego okekan fimi Arundu

One who slices garden egg and

swallows Arundu

Ayi lere oooo
(Name of masquerade)
Ayi lere oooo
Ayi lere oooo

Aro badara oooo
(Name of masquerade)
Egungun ile wa oooo
Ancestors of our lineage, ooo
Adegboro ye oooo
(Name of masquerade)
Begungun yo woso asiri ba
When a masquerade want to put on
cloth, he first pays homage to the
ancestors

Iba oooooo
Homage, ooooo
Moriba fun baba mi

Homage to you my father

Baba mi

My father

Eni ile o gbe

one who would be favored on earth

Iba ooo

Homage, ooooo

Moriba fun baba mi

Homage to you my father

Osun

Kiki *Oreyeye osun ooo*

Goodness, Mother Osun

Osun oreyeye ooooo

Goodness, Mother Osun

Orin *Ek'oreyeye ooooooo*

Shout oreyeye ooo

Ek'oreyeye osun

Shout oreyeye ooo

Olomo ni ya ooooo

Mother of children

Olomo ni ya wa

My mother is the mother of children

Oriki *Ajeje iya oni*

Ajeje the mother of the day

Aladekoju

Owner of the beautiful crown

Amo awomoro

She knows the secrets but does not tell

O wa yarin yarin kowo si

She, who digs the soil and keeps money

there

Ole wawa wa korowo

She, who digs the soil and keeps money
there

Emi rowomoro mofaikupariwa

I dig and find money, children and longevity

Awede wemo

She who washes bracelets and children

Yeye olomo lokiti efon

My mother of children in Okiti Efon village

Ose Ngese

The Ose Ngese

Iyami oke bale

My mother in Oke Bale

Abimo mojayale

One who gave birth without labor

Alagbolodo

One who has herbs in the river

Alagbo lodo iku ole pomotofun mi

mother who has herb in river, her given
child would have longevity

Orí

Kiki   *Ori huuuuu*

Exalted praises to Orí

Ori huuuuuuu

Exalted praises to Orí

Orin   *Mo wa bori mi oooooo*

I come to feed my orí

Kori mi le dayo x2

so that my ori will bring my joy

Mo mun [agbon] wa bori mi koriledayo

I use [name materials] to feed my orí for joy

Origbalu o gbajo ogbara

Orí accept the kolanut once ogbara ngada x2

Ori kore gbogbo wa ogbarangada

Orí, may all blessings come, ogbara ngada

Ori gbobi lowo kan ogbara n gada x2

Orí, accept the obi divination on the first throw

Oriki   *Ori huuuuu*

Exalted praises to Orí

ori apere

Orí of apere

atakara sewa

One who sells the bean cake to the honourable

adaniwaye mogbagbe eni

One who created us and supported us

atete niran atete gbeniju

The one always remembers us

ori loda oya sile ra

It is you created Oya at Ile Ira

ori loda sango si koso

It is you created Sango at Koso town

ori loda esu odara sile ketu

It is you created Esu Odara at Ketu

atata ni gogo

The Atata Nigogo

atoni gbe mope eni kan

It is enough to favour us without any other intervention

ori olowo mo koo mora ooo

Orí of riches, I embrace you

ori otosi pada leyin mi ooooo

Orí of impoverishment, get behind me

Obatala

Kiki   *heepaa oosa*

The Greatest Òrìsà

oosa heepa

Òrìsà, the Greatest

Orin   *orisanla alaba alase oooo*

Orisanla, the authority

moyin atata gorigo ooo x2

I praise you, special being x2

Oriki   *orisanla alaba alase*

Orisanla, the authority

atata gorigo

The Atata Gorigo

iku ike

The ambassador of death

baba arugbo

the eldest

jagin ile n bade

The warrior of Bade's house

agbalowo nini gba fun aini

He who receives from one who has plenty

o so eni kan di gba eni

He who receives from one who has plenty

oosanla oni ka ninu

He multiplies one person into a thousand and one

o gbe soso boju aseni

Orisa is not wicked but put a sharp stick to the eye an evil doer

o ti ese elegbo bo ajiyan eerun

Orisanla, the Osere of Igbo puts a wounded leg to the soldier ant

oosa nla osere igbo logbe ana re

so sinu oti gbigbona

Oosa nla osere igbo put his wicked in-law into hot liquor

heepa oosa

Heepa oosa

Òrunmìlà

Aboru Aboye

May the sacrifice be performed, may it be accepted

Aboye Abosise

May the sacrifice be accepted, may it manifest

Orin   *igi larere ifa gba wa oooo x2*

Arere is an important tree

Ifa a mu eku ,eja oti eran looo

Ifa, we bring fish, rat and goat

Awa fi beyin oooo

All for appeasement to you

Igi larere ifa gba wa ooooo x2

Arere is an important tree x2

Olomo nini ifa gba wa oooo x2

Olomonini, Ifa please save us x2

je ki ile aye roju

Let the world be settled

tori pe orun o julo

Because heaven is difficult to go

orunmila da bo

Please Òrunmìlà

omo enire

The son of Enire

omo kanin kanin janirenire

The son of a sponge which breaks completely

apanile olu si

The apa in the house of olusi

igede ni le oduduwa

Igede in Oduduwa's house

ifa olokun asorodayo

Ifá changes bad situations into good ones

o to bajaye mojaye lo lo

The one you can move with, and not regret it

akere fogbon senu

Small, but filled with knowledge

okinkin ti meyin erinfon

Okinkin in the elephant's house

omo eekannan owo komekun hora

son of the fingernail that does not allow
tiger to scratch its body

ewi ile ado

The Ewi of Ado kingdom

erin mi ode òwò

The Erinmi of Owo kingdom

omo ele polopo oje adi

one who has plenty of palm oil and refused
to take adi

heepa nile ifa ooooo

Praise to Ifá!

Ogun

Kiki *ogun ye*

Ogun develops (himself)

mo ye

I develop (myself)

ogun yee

Ogun develops (himself)

Orin *oko ti molo oooo*

the farm that I visited

ti mo mu re bo

and I returned with prosperity

ogun modupe

Ogun, I thank you

ogun lakaye

the ogun lakaye

onija ole

the strongest fighter

ejemu oniwonran

the ejemun of wonran village

adigirigiri rebi ija

the one clever in fighting

koko eti odo ti ro minimini

the river bank grass sounds gently

egbe leyin omo kan

he favors lonely children

egbe leyin omo adaloro

he favors the orphan

onile kangunkangun ona orun

the owner of shapeless houses in the heaven

mo ni ogun onire oko mi

I said ogun onire, my husband!

mo ni meje logun mi

I said there are seven Ogun of mine

ogun alara nijaja

Ogun alara eats dog

oni onire won a jagbo

Ogun onire eats ram

ogun ikola ni je gbin

Ogun ikola eats snail

ogun molamola ni yekuru funfun

Ogun molamola eats white baked beans

ogun gbondogbondo eja ni je

Ogun gbondogbondo eats fish

ogun onigbaja mo irunnije

Ogun oni gbajamo eats hair

ogun alapata ni jeje eran

Ogun alapata eats animal blood

ojumo oni mo kalapata momoje eje eran

Butcher always eats animal blood every blessed day

eji gbojo omo yawukotoyagi

Ejigbojo who breaks the smithy before breaking tree

atamunyan alagbe abi emin selele

Atamunyan the blacksmith who has the razor scissors

Ibeji

Kiki	*E n le oooooo*
	Hello, ooo
	Ejire
	Double blessings
	Ara isokun
	Indigene of Isokun
Orin	*Edun loni njo maajo x2*
	Edun asks me to dance and I dance x2
	Emi o le tori ijo komo
	I will never refuse my child because of dancing
	Edun loni njo majo
	Edun asks me to dance and I dance
	Emi o le torijo komo
	I will never refuse my child because of dancing
Oriki	*E dun jobi*
	Identical twins
	Ejire ara isokan
	Ejire from isokun village

Edun eleyinju ege

Edun, the visionary

ologungun apero

The Ologungun Aparan

Ikan ni iyalohun yio bi eji loyale wa

I planned to give birth to one and twins came

Win ni wini loju orogun

Little in the eye of enemy

Ejiworo loju iya ee

Formless twins in their mother's eye

Obe kisi bekese

The clever jumper

O be sile alakisa

who jumps to the poor family

O so di onigba aso

And makes them rich

Edun eleyin ito Sanran saram saran labe aso

Edun, who has the sharp teeth under the cloth

Omo taye wole wa ooooooo

Omotaye, come in!

Komomo gbeyin erelu omo ki gbe eyin ekun

Don't hold back

Omo kanhunde wole waoooo

Because a good child will not be at the back door

Komomo gbeyin erelu omo ki gbeyin ooooo

Don't hold back

Because a good child will not be at the back door

Sàngó

Kiki   Kabiyesi sango

Your highness, Sango!

Kabiyesi sango

Your highness, Sango!

Orin   Omo kekere mosokele oooo

Children, I tied up my okele necklace

Mosokele

I tied up my okele necklace

Agbalagba mosokole oooooo

Elders, I tied up my okele necklace

Mosokele

I tied up my okele necklace

Sango, mosomilokun lofun

Sango please don't tie rope on my neck

Mosokele

I tied up my okele necklace

Oriki   Olukoso ooo

Lord of Koso

Ahayana

The brightest light

Inaloju

Fire in the eyes

Inalemu

Fire in the mouth

Inalorule

Fire on the roof

Sagiri lagiri

Breaking down walls

Olagiri paapaa fi gba edu bo

Breaking down walls completely with 200
thunderbolts

Ina ni gbegenge ti fi kun igi

He climbs the tree carrying light and fire

Oke kara kekoro

He sounds loudly and heavily

To soloro di jin ni jinni

One who makes the coward comply

Arabambi onigba oja

Arabambi of thousand of stones

Ewelere oba koso

The medicine maker King of koso

Gbegiri ooo

Gbegiri soup, ooo

Epo yio dun be ooooo

It makes the soup sweet, ooo

Oya

Kiki *Heepa Oya ooo*

Hail mighty Oya ooo

Oya oriri!

Oya oriri!

Orin *Olupo Ala elu*

Distinguished person from Ala Elu village

Ewa wo oya

Come and see Oya

O fun mi lomo bi

One who brought me children

Ewa wo oya

Come and see Oya

Iya a n san somidolowo

Mother of Nine, She leads me to riches

Ewa wo oya

Come and see Oya

He he he oro!!!

Oya ooo!

Oya oriri!

Oriki   *Oya Okara*

Oya of Okara village

Adadu loyan

She made a drum from her breast

Alafefe ina

Owner of fiery winds

Alawotele oorun

Her underwear is full of sunshine

Oya iya a n san

Oya, mother of nine

Oya pele o

Gently, Oya

O Je ogan legbe

You destroy the wasp's house (powerful)

Oya pele o

Gently, Oya

Je ogan legbe

You destroy the wasp's house (powerful)

Iya mi

My mother

Afefe nla ti ngbagi gbaju

Heavy storm that shake tree and bush

Efufu legelege ti gbara we

Heavy wind that blows away litter

Oya olupo ara alailu

Oya Olupo the owner of Ala Ilu town

Oya Opere

Oya of Opere

ekun oko aseke

a leopard that despises traitors

Olupo Ala Ilu

Olupo Ala Ilu

Ewa wo oya o

Come and see Oya

Afefe nla gbagi gbarawe

Heavy storm that blows away trees and blows away litter

E wa wo oya

Come and see Oya

Odù

Kiki	*Hepa odu*
	Greatest reverence, Odù!
	Odu heap
	Odù, greatest reverence!
Orin	*Ifa o tona ooo*
	Ifa is not lice
	Oduo tero
	Odu is not lice
	Ebora ti gba omo nihun-ni
	But the orisa who grants favors and success
Oriki	*Odu seki alagba oje*
	Odu seki who has the lead barrel
	Aronibi oba
	She who makes one king
	Eleyinyu otingin ni
	One with the horrible face
	Anire ni wa
	The prosperous and kind one
	Aniwalanu

The well behaved and merciful one

Eleyingu ege

One with the attractive face

Obele mewa

The Obele mewa

Osa tilamo

The orisa who makes one successful

Osa tigbemo

The orisa who favors one

Osa ti pa asebi

The orisa who kills the wicked

Egbe

Kiki   *Akiika*

Aseege

Oro yikasi ara oooo

The issue is logical

Ole momo rimo ooo

It is mysterious

Orin   *Omo elegbe ni wa ooooo*

I am the offspring of Egbe's spirit

Omo elegbe ni wa ooo he

I am the offspring of Egbe's spirit

Aisoje ka so ju ti mi

One cannot be Oje's child and be ashamed

Omo elegbe ni wa

I am the offspring of Egbe's spirit

E je n begbemi jo oooo he

Let me be with my spirit

E jen begbemi pe o ha

Let me be with my spirit

E je n begbemi pe o heeeee

Let me be with my spirit

Aisoje ka soju ti mi o ooo

One cannot be Oje's child and be ashamed

Ejen begbe mi pe

Let me be with my spirit

Oriki   *Egbe oga ogo*

Egbe, the master of glory

A to elesin tele

One capable of following horse rider

Apo jojo bii erupe

Uncountable like sand

Eleriko subu

Eleriko subu

Borokinni aye

The influential one on earth

Borokinni orun

The influential one in heaven

Ara orita mo peyin

The cross-road spirit, I call you

Ara idi iroko mo peyin

The spirits of iroko tree, I call you

Ara inu esun mo peyin

The spirits of the grass, I call you

Egbe maahun, maahun

Egbe maahun maahun

Iyalode Abaabe

The strong woman of Abaabe

Ofigele teripa ooo

Who dangles headgear on her head

Elerin mosa aso

Elerin mosa aso

Orere woye

Orere woye

Ebami damu so fun Egbé

Help me give kudos to Egbé

Yemoja

Kiki	*Omi ooo*
	Water, ooo
	Eri ooo
	Stream, ooo
Orin	*Oluweri iwo loba lomi 2X*
	Oluweri, you are the queen in the water
	Omomo somi lodo mo ooo
	There is no other queen in the water, except you
	Oluweri iwo loba lomi
	Oluweri, you are the queen in the water
	Komo mo somi lodo mo ooo
	There is no other queen in the water, except you
	Iyemoja iwo loba lomi
	Iyemoja you are the queen in the water
Oriki	*Oluweri mogbeti*
	Oluweri who never dries
	Iyemoja awoyo

Iyemoja of complete beauty

Iyemoja toni ibu

Iyemoja owner of the main river

Oni penpeju omi

Owner of eyes filled with water

Asanlugbulugbu mo tan 2X

Asanlugbu lugbu mo tan

Arugbo odo

Eldest river

Ogbere gbere

Ogbere gbere

Ojetu je pepeye

She who eats guinea fowl, eats duck

Mojelewi

Mojelewi

Eleja kaa keni sowo

The owner of blessed fish

Olomi amu sola

The owner of a nurturing water

Olomi amu kemi

The owner of honored water

Olomi amu seye

The owner of resourceful water

Yeye mi

My mother

Iyemoja

Iyemoja

ari bowo fun

of honour

Sonponna

Kiki	*Atoto arere ooo*
	Straighten up!
	Obaluaiye mo n rin ooo
	Obaluaye is on his way
Orin	*Atoto ooooo, atoto arere 2x,*
	Straighten up!
	Obaluaye mo n rin bo
	Obaluaye is on his way
	atoto ooooo
	Straighten up!
Oriki	*Obaluaiye*
	Obaluaiye
	Oni wowo ado
	The owner of plenty gourds
	Arumoloogun danu
	He who renders charms useless
	Aramonda
	A unique man
	Elerankun ti n damoniji lojuorun

Thread maker who performs miracles in dreams

Ajagajigi Sanponna

Ajagajigi Sanponna

Onikumo kan a fi le, oran lo

An archer who uses arrows to display problems

Elewon ojiji

The chain owner who awakens people

Baba mole

A genius of a man

Abi ewo gereje lorun

One with large attire

Obaluaiye mo n rin oooo

Obaluaye is on his way

Olokun

Kiki *Omi ooo*

Water, ooo

Eri ooo

Stream, ooo

Orin *Mo wo iwaju Olokun... Rere!*

I look before Olokun... Limitless!

Rere ningba oooo! Rere!

Unlimited flow!

Mo weyin Olokun... Rere!

I look behind Olokun... Limitless

Rere ningba o. Rere!

Unlimited flow!

Oriki *Olokun aje ti aye oba omi*

Olokun a life without end

Omi nla to kari aye

King of water

Osele gbe senibu omi

Great water that covers the whole world

Ti koni momo

A wonderful ocean that has no end

Gbogbo eni ti waje

Who ever wants wealth

E je ka kori sile olokun

Let them go to Olokun's house

Sanle aje

Who has uncountable wealth

Baba eni to laje 2X

Father of uncountable wealth

Ogbugu ni so oni so boji

One who has abundant wealth

Alagbalu gbu omi 2X

Water without end

Eni ajiki

He who we greet early

Eni ajike

He welcome and receive well

Ai ri di Olokun

Nobody knows the source of Olokun

Ao mo bere re

No one knows his beginning

Aje pe gbogbo omi

Let all water bow down for Olokun

Efi ori fun olokun gbogbo odo

Because Olokun is the head of all rivers

E fi ori fun olokun oba omi

Because olokun is the head, king of waters

Omi ooooooooo

Water oooooooo

Òrìsà Oko

E se Ode ni hin

Welcome Ode from hunting

Ah hin ha e se ode ni hin

A hunter's greeting!

Orisa oko pele pele dowo re 2X

Òrìsà Oko please, protect us

Omo to fun wa ko gbodo ku o,

Don't the child you have brought us die

Orisa oko pelepele dowo re

Òrìsà Oko please, protect us

Orisa oko ake fon

Orisa oko ake fon

Suugudu alawo oloto

Suugudu a being with beautiful complexion

Aditi fe ti dele

A deaf one who uses his ears to hear from home (a long distance)

Ode ogongo ti rin tomitomi

Hunter of Ogongo who runs with water

O ba ologi gun ogi

He who helps one to grind corn

O ba eleko gun eko

He who helps one to make pap

O sanu eleko

He who helps the pap owner

Lojekopa egbefa

To profit Egbefa

Oba sii gi

The king of Siigi

Oba re gi

The king of Regi

E sode ni hin

A hunter's greeting!

Oduduwa

Kiki   *Iba Oodua ooo*

Homage to Oduduwa

Odua iba

Oduduwa, homage to you

Orin   *Ero wa oooo Oduduwa ooo*

Descend, oh! Oduduwa

E wa gbe waooo

Come and bless us

e gbe wa sowo

Come and bless us with money

Ero wa o Oduduwa ooo

Descend, oh! Odududuwa

E wa gbe ooo

Come and bless us

kasi lowo

Favor us with money

lowo ero wa ooo Oduduwa

With money descend among us, Oduduwa

Oriki   *Iba re Oduduwa*

I pay homage to Oduduwa

Atewon ro ni ife

One who descends upon a chain to Ife

Olofin akoko

The first Olofin

Olofin risa

Olofin of the deities

Ajalaye

The one who controls the earth

Aja lorun

The one who has power in heaven

Agbodiwon ran

The deity of immortality

Oba olofin, ala roro bi ala

King Olofin in white cloth

Oba alajiki

The first greeted king

Oba alajige

The king whom people care for

Oba agbayegun

The one who sustains the world

Iba re Oduduwa

I pay homage to Oduduwa

Atewon ro ni ife

One who descends upon a chain to Ife

Bayan ni/Dada

Kiki   *Dada Olowo eyo*

Dada, the custodian of cowries

Orin   *Bayan ni olowo eyo*

Bayan ni, the custodian of cowries

Ero iju sele n bo lona ooo

The forest crowd is coming

Bayan ni olowo eyo

Bayan ni, the custodian of cowries

Oriki   *Orisa bayan ni*

Orisa bayan ni

Orisa Dada

Orisa Dada

Ajaka ekun

Ajaka ekun

Dada olowo eyo

Dada, the custodian of cowries

Bi iju sele di ga ga ga

How ever crowded the forest may be

Bi iju sele di pin pin pin

How ever dry the forest may look

Bi iju sele di pin pin pin
How ever dry the forest may look
Bayan ni a alana owo fun eni to fe
Bayan ni will open the door of wealth
Lana owo aye yii kan mi
For whom ever he wants to bless
Ero iju sele
The crowded forest